Dedication

In memory of the Victims of

the September 11th Tragedy.

Their lives were not lost,

they were given;

so that everything we had lost

could be recovered.

The Invisible Enemy

our war against terror

The Invisible Enemy

our war against terror

Dwayne N. Hunt

Grace Publishing
Memphis, TN 38109

THE INVISIBLE ENEMY
our war against terror

Published by
Grace Publishing, Memphis, Tennessee 38109

Cover Illustration by
Craig Thompson, Disciple Design, Memphis, TN
Photography by Phillip Parker

For information or to schedule speaking engagements:
Dwayne N. Hunt * 843 W. Raines Rd * Memphis, TN 38109
1-877-88-GRACE
www.theinvisibleenemy.org
www.dwaynehunt.com

ISBN 1-893555-36-4

Contents

"FEAR IS THE MOST DESTRUCTIVE
FORCE IN THE WORLD TODAY.
IT IS MUCH EASIER TO
FRIGHTEN PEOPLE,
AND MORE PROFITABLE,
THAN TO PERSUADE THEM."
- WALTER STONE

CHAPTER ONE

Airplanes and Airmail

On September 11, 2001 our world as we knew it, changed. As a result of the terrorist attacks that day, President George W. Bush made a declaration of war. The news media has defined it as America's New War. One reason it is called a "New War" is because the enemy is not clearly defined. Normally, war is a conflict between nations or a military campaign between armies. However, in this particular case, the question has been asked, "On whom have we declared war?" There is a person that we say is responsible for the genocide, but it is unheard of for a nation to declare war on one individual. This New War is actually more against a 'what' than a 'who'.

This declaration of war is made against Terrorism. That means we are fighting an "ism". Unlike the "isms" in past wars - such as Fascism or Communism, this is more than an ideology. **Terrorism is a method**. In that light, this new war requires that we learn new warfare methods and develop new warfare strategies.

During the Vietnam War, we failed to make the proper military and mental adjustments needed for a new type of conflict: guerrilla warfare. It pitted our highly skilled and equipped army against an irregular enemy, lacking in comparable strength, but highly motivated and chameleon-like in their native environment. That enemy, without defining uniforms, blended into the jungles and villages, making them difficult to distinguish and attack, and even more difficult to capture. For the record, against that unorthodox foe, our superior army lost.

Now, in this New War against terrorism, although the enemy is not indigenous, he has successfully infiltrated and blended into our social tapestry. He has learned to adapt to our culture and community, yet maintain his intense hatred for the society that absorbs him. In this New War, our enemy walks openly among us, yet *he is invisible.*

(As an aftermath of the horrific events, there are accounts of retaliatory attacks by Americans against people of Arabic origin, Muslim faith and Middle-Eastern dress. Those assaults are not just racist; they are ridiculous, because the people that we would have reason to fear are not those who would distinguish themselves or stand out. The ones to fear are those who have strategically learned *not* to draw any attention to themselves. The real enemy successfully blends in, never raising a suspicion that they are a threat to our personal or homeland security.)

Our government has announced that the war on terrorism will be fought on many fronts, and to win, it must be waged with a combination of conventional and non-conventional forces. The first shots our government fired in this battle were with banks, not bazookas, freezing terrorists' financial assets. Coalition building, diplomatic persuasion and foreign policy have become as important as Pentagon planning. Intelligence gathering and federal law enforcement technology have been just as critical as military muscle. While F-18s drop bombs on Afghanistan, C-17s drop bread as humanitarian aid supports air strikes.

However, this multi-faceted war on terrorism is not comprehensive unless it includes the Church. The Spiritual element must be included to ensure any type of total victory, as the Church has the only army trained and skilled at fighting *an invisible enemy*.

President Bush clearly defined who the invisible enemy is and why the Church must be included in the war: "We are at the beginning of what I view as a very long struggle against evil. We're not fighting a nation. We're not fighting a religion. We're fighting evil."

By positioning the Church in the middle of this conflict, I am not saying that this is a "holy war". Although the Taliban has declared that this is now a "Jihad", or "holy war" and the president, himself, has referred to this new conflict as a "crusade". What *I am* saying is that the events of September 11th and the subsequent actions to spread terror through the mail are of demonic origin, thus, there must be a Spiritual response. The motivating element in this warfare can only be fought using Spiritual weapons. **Our superior, conventional army is not equipped to fight a war in the**

realm of the Spirit.

The declaration itself, "The War on Terrorism", communicates to us that this is a Spiritual war. The word "terror" is translated in the scripture and in the dictionary as "overwhelming fear". Fear, itself, is 'an emotion, caused by a sense of danger'. So, we are waging a war against internal, invisible forces. Victory in The War Against Terrorism means winning the battle over the power of an emotion. **Our superior conventional army is not equipped to fight that war against terror and fear.**

Fear is a cruel and cunning enemy. It is a great thief that comes to sap the strength of our soul, then hold us captive. On September 11th, it stole our sense of security. We were robbed of our innocence, as we became witnesses to the mass murder of thousands. The violent events revisited us in the nights to steal our sleep; replacing it with night-terrors, panic attacks, and post-traumatic stress. Where we once felt safe and untouchable, we now feel frightened, vulnerable, powerless and uncertain.

Fear refused to let us rest. Terror did not give us a moment to grieve our losses or recover the remains of our loved ones from the ashes. While we were still grappling with the reality that our airplanes had been transformed into deadly missiles, suddenly our airmail became transmitters of deadly microorganisms.

Just as we began The New War Against Terrorism on one front, we came under a sinister attack by *another* unseen enemy. **This new invisible enemy launched his attacks against us using an invisible substance**. These hideous assaults were made by launching lethal, unseen anthrax spores into the air. These spores can attach to the skin or, worse, be inhaled with normal breathing.

The things that *were* common and ordinary before September 11th, now evoke anxiety and alarm. What we all handle daily has now become deadly, for this new invisible enemy delivers death through powdered postage.

In the shadow of these atrocities, we are no longer just suspicious of people with brown skin, beards and headdress; our anxiousness has us paranoid of powdery substances and parcel post. Our apprehension has made us consider stockpiling antibiotics and storing gas masks. Our fears have set off many false alarms and have removed the oddity from seeing people in 'Haz-Mat suits'. We have put stress on our emergency response services <u>and</u> on our emotional response sensors, as any-little-thing now scares us.

Adding to our fears is the knowing that our enemies have found refuge by hiding in the open. They are among us, yet invisible.

In spite of being a "Superpower", we were unprepared for these new enemies in this New War, using new weapons. They have taken the things that we are most familiar with, things that we would never suspect, and used it against us. Never before had a commercial airline been turned into a guided missile. This was also the first time that anthrax has successfully been used as a bio-weapon. However, the *principle weapon* being used against us is not new, we are only experiencing new implementations of old, old weapons — terror and fear!

The success of using these old weapons is that they have been proven to linger in the air to torment the mind, long after the violent or vile incidents have been committed by the terrorists. The strength of fear and terror goes beyond the realities of danger; it is the *imagination* of a sudden, horrific thing that *could* happen. It allows the enemy to dominate, *not because of* *his* *power, but because of* *our* *imagination.* (2 Corinthians 10:4-5)

Then, fear begins to limit and control our lives. Already, our anticipation of future terrorist assaults has paralyzed us, restricting our movement. The travel industry has been devastated by our fears to the price tag of billions of dollars. The plummeting stock market, in the weeks immediately following the first attack, was the barometer of our depression. We have lost what it means to "breathe easy", as we open our mail with trepidation. It was only a short time ago when our greatest concerns about viruses in the mail were related to the computer. Now it seems trivial to worry about crashing hard drives, after being eyewitness to crashing planes. Now it is not as significant that you can lose information on your PC because of an email virus, while those handling hard mail are losing their lives.

Overwhelmed by the events and the information, we have become an anxiety-ridden nation.

The outrageous acts of terrorism are more than attacks on symbols of our capitalistic system and on our government. They are attacks on our very soul. Terror is a greater enemy than the terrorists; for terror continues to wreak havoc long after the terrorist act is over. As horrific as the events of September 11th were, the loss of life and collateral damage was minimal, if this is a war. **It is the psychological damage inflicted by the enemy that has taken the greatest toll.** That is the victory of terror and fear.

Terror and fear are not just evil. They are principle devices of The Evil One, according to the Bible, the Torah <u>and</u> the Qur'an. They have been a part of his arsenal long before there was an Osama bin Laden or a Genghis Khan or an Attila the Hun. Through the ages, weaponry and military technology have changed, but terror has remained his primary weapon.

Terror works because it takes the fight to an unseen plane — inside of you, in your mind, in your soul. That is why I so boldly place the Church in the middle of this fight. For, while the battleground against *terrorists* may be in the Middle East, and the battlefront against *terrorism* may be in mail facilities, the battlefield against *terror* is in the mind. There the campaign must be fought and there it must be won.

Against terror and fear, our military might

pales. As great as our army is, it is ill-equipped to take on those enemies, for they are internal, intangible and invisible. Our armed forces may be able to subdue the perpetrators of the horrors, but they cannot overcome the sorrow of the soul.

And when the physical war is over, victory has been declared and the troops have been called home, those warriors must deal with their own sorrow of the soul. It once went by the name of "Shell-Shock". Whether it was the shells or the horrors, it left our heroes in "shock". As we have progressed in our diagnosis, it now goes by the name of "Post-Traumatic Stress Disorder". Whatever it is called, any veteran of combat will tell you that when the war is over, the fight against the internal enemy continues.

This internal, invisible enemy is most dangerous, because long after his seen representatives have been vanquished, his spores of fear remain to *'torment you'* (1 John 4:18). Infected by his deadly virus of terror, it spreads throughout the whole of your being, causing the hallucination of danger where there is none. This infection and its hallucinations cannot be cured with medication. This enemy is spiritual and can only be overcome by Spiritual forces. **The Church must fight that battle.**

One thing that especially equips the Church to battle on that plane is our military manual: The Holy Bible. It is the most thorough book on the use of conventional warfare in combination with Spiritual tactics. It gives military strategy on both the natural and Spiritual theatres of war. It is replete with training and instructions that equip us for this New War Against Terrorism. This warriors' handbook transcends the military strategies taught by West Point and Annapolis. It prepares and equips the members of the Church's standing army to fight against the spirit forces of fear and terror, and to be victorious over the invisible enemy.

We find a portion of this preparation in The Book of Jeremiah, Chapter 6, Verses 24-26. The Prophet actually gives a discourse on terrorism. It speaks not just to the acts of terrorism, but even the affects of the news reporting of the terrorist events. That is very relevant and significant to our case here in America. The majority of Americans have been exposed to the events through the news and, thank God, not *physically* exposed to the terrorist acts, themselves. That is not to say that we have not been affected, because we have been, greatly. It is to show that we can find a specific case, applicable to our own in the Scriptures.

Jeremiah then addresses how the shock of what we saw on the news overwhelmed our emotions. I refer to it as the *depressive regression.* It is what happens as the events begin to be filtered through our senses, then down through our emotions. Then as our emotions send signals back to our body, we experience physical reactions such as crying, sweating, hand ringing, chest pain, heart palpitations, muscle tension and shortness of breath.

Those physiological reactions and tensions are minor compared to the psychological toll taken on the soul. *"Anguish"* is how Jeremiah describes it; pain and torment of the soul. All because of an act of terror.

He then shows us the social effects and behavioral changes that occur. We see how constraining the acts of terrorism can be on our ordinary daily life. It restricts our movement, narrows our world and limits our relationships. We isolate ourselves, lending to depression and paranoia.

Finally, Jeremiah addresses the lingering torment of fear and how that emotion continues to harass us, long after the external enemy has been expelled. We are still held captive by the debilitating anticipation of future terror:

> "We have heard reports about them,
> and our hands hang limp.
> Anguish has gripped us,
> pain (has come upon us suddenly)
> like that of a woman in labor.
> Do not go out to the fields
> or walk on the roads,
> for the enemy has a sword,
> and there is terror on every side.
> O my people, put on sackcloth
> and roll in ashes;
> mourn with bitter wailing as for an only son,
> for suddenly the destroyer
> will come upon us." (NIV)

Jeremiah shows us what we have now learned firsthand, that the objective of terrorism is to use the anticipation of future evils to torment the mind, completely change the way we live, and make the fear of a future terrorist attack our constant companion. Simply put, those strategies are demonic, and that is why the Church must step into its critical position in this conflict.

This is just a sampling of what is in the Church's Field Manual on the subject of terrorism. The Church has this information because we are expected to be the principals in engaging this spirit enemy.

From the beginning, our response to the reports of terrorism should not parallel the responses described in Jeremiah. Ours should be different from that of the general population: *"He will have no fear of bad news; his heart is steadfast, trusting in the LORD. His heart is secure, he will have no fear; in the end he will look in triumph on his foes"* (Ps 112:7-8 NIV).

The reports of terrorism should have generated an immediate war cry in the Church, instead of lament alone. It should have stirred our righteous rage. We knew who the perpetrator was when others were still making assumptions. We recognized his methods and his M.O. (modus operandi). That, alone, should have stirred us to the fight, for this was our old, unseen enemy. For the Church, this is not a New War Against Terrorism, but the continuation of an old, old struggle against terror.

As we will clearly see in future chapters, the Church is uniquely empowered on the inside for this internal battle against this invisible enemy: *"For God has not given us a spirit of fear, but of power and of love and of a sound mind"* (2 Tim 1:7 NKJV).

Hugh Black adds, "The fear of God kills all other fears."

As we address our fight against fear, please bear this in mind: It is a very different struggle to keep from being overcome by fear than it is to fight to overcome fear, itself. As individuals, we basically fight to keep fear from overcoming us. The Church must take its position on the frontline to assault fear at its root – in the Spirit realm. The Church must overcome fear!

Reveille sounded the morning of September 11th. The Church received a "call to arms". We must be fearless and "Advance!" For only the Church can lead in the fight against *terror* and *fear*. Only the Church can defeat ***The Invisible Enemy***!

"SINCE, THEREFORE,
THE FEAR OF DEATH
IS THE MOTHER OF ALL FEARS,
WHEN IT HAS BEEN DESTROYED,
ALL OTHER FORMS OF FEAR
ARE THEREBY VANQUISHED."
- JOHN SUTHERLAND BONNELL

CHAPTER TWO

Before I Wake

Terrorist operations do not rely on numerical strength. **Their principle strength is in the psychological after-affects of their shocking, violent acts**. The terrorists do not position themselves to be our worst enemy. They make our greatest enemy *our own* fears.

They don't have to kill us. They can just scare us to death!

Fear, in itself, is a normal, natural emotion. It is God-given for our protection. Fear prevents you from walking off a ledge or sticking our hand into a fire. It can warn you of danger present or impending. Fear can save your life.

Fear is also connected to your experiences and your memory. There, it works not only as an emotion, but also as a reflex action. Affixed to your experiences, fear responds to pain and to traumatic events. After processing the experiences, it then instructs you to avoid certain situations or certain people, thus protecting you from future trauma and pain.

However, fear unabated moves from the role of being a **protector** to being a **preventer**. After interpreting the events, it acts to prevent you from anything else that might induce or 'trigger' more feelings of fear. It is difficult to resist because its reasoning is strong and its offer of safety seems irresistible. All the while it is really preventing you from truly living. It prevents you from exploring and growing. It slowly begins to close the door to the wonders and possibilities of life, securing you in a dark, dull, but *safe* room.

That is when you move from a natural fear to *"a spirit of fear"* (2 Tim 1:7).

Then fear progresses, actually I should say regresses, in its role from preventer to **controller**. It acts to control and manipulate your environment. It puts up fences to keep scary stuff and scary people out, but it is really keeping you in. It puts up a safety net supposedly to prevent you from falling, but it actually ensnares you. It *contains* you in the name of *caution.*

From being a controller, fear regresses to being a **tormentor**. It consumes your mind with persistent thoughts and recurring images that only feed your anxiety. It constantly rehearses to the mind the negative possibilities of what *could* happen. It predicts and prophesies the worst.

Then fear secures itself in your soul by offering to protect you from the things *it* has only imagined. Even though you may not consciously welcome the fear, you embrace it because it tells you that it is your only protector.

All the while, fear is killing your spirit. It does this while presenting the 'rationale' that it is protecting you from life's worst fate — death. That is where the seduction of fear finds firm footing and causes so much torment — in the fear of death.

That is where torment turns to **terror**. You become terrified that something terrible will happen to you, the worst of which would be death.

Thus, the one thing in life that is most inevitable is the one thing that you are afraid of most.

Because of that single dread, our enemies are able to turn what is natural in you, against you, and make your greatest enemy *your own* fear.

It is our fear of death that the enemy manipulates to his distinct advantage. He can manipulate that fear because he doesn't share it. This is how a band of less than 20 terrorists can send tremors of terror throughout a nation of more than 280 million. Not only were they not afraid to die, they counted it a duty and a privilege to become martyrs for their cause. They touched the greatest fear of Americans: the fear of death.

Let's face it: it was not just the attacks that scared us. It was the realization that those men willingly sacrificed their lives that made their actions all the more frightening. That let us know that there are no limitations to what they are willing to do for their cause.

As we watched the horrors of September 11th unfold, I was gravely reminded of Revelations 12:11: *"They overcame him because of the blood of the Lamb and because of the word of their testimony, and **they did not love their life even when faced with death**"* (NASU). Those terrorists were willing to give their lives to overcome their perceived enemy. This characteristic belongs to the victorious Church and overcoming Christians, according to the Word of God.

What they tried to use as their advantage, is the Church's birthright – no fear in death! The Christian legacy is that our Savior, Jesus Christ, was nailed to a cross by terrorists. Our victory is guaranteed in that Christ Jesus was resurrected, triumphing over death and the grave. Our testimony is that our living Lord took the "sting" away from death. Our hope is in life – *His* life, *this* life and the eternal life to come, along with its glorious reward for being victorious over the invisible enemy.

With that confidence, we can live with purpose. Even in this new age of terrorism, when seemingly the *"shadow of death"* looms, we can live without *"a spirit of fear"*.

A victim of terrorism in the first century, Jesus teaches us to have an attitude that will bring amazement to our enemy: *"Do not be afraid of those who kill the body but cannot kill the soul. Rather, be afraid of the One who can destroy both soul and body in hell"* (Matt 10:28 NIV).

The enemy can *only* kill the body. When we

understand that our bodies are just clay containers, already in the process of deteriorating, and that the Bible cautions us against being too attached to them, then we can echo Paul of Tarsus: *"none of these things move me; nor do I count my life dear to myself"* (Acts 20:24 NKJV).

When *this* Christian disposition becomes a part of our very being, **we actually disarm the enemy, taking away his power to use fear and death as weapons against us.** Our courageous stand turns his tools against him, causing fear to invade his heart. Thus, he is not able to fulfill his objective of making us cower and come under his control.

As a matter of fact, our Field Manual gives us explicit directions as to how we are to deal with terrorists and terrorism. We have standing orders which state that *we are not to be, in any way, terrified by our adversaries.* Our ability to stand in the face of the enemy, without any fear, *"is a sign to them that they will be destroyed"* (Phil 1:28 NIV).

The most critical piece of information, in preparation to engage our invisible enemy, is the knowledge that Jesus Christ has already won the decisive battle. In His victory, He dealt the crushing blow to the enemy! So, we are fighting a wounded, defeated foe, who doesn't even have his own weapons. Think about it. The enemy's plan involves using our own emotions against us, just as they had to hijack, then use our own planes and mail against us. The term for that is *Emotional Hijacking*.

We must begin to fight back to recover our soul from the "spirit of fear". **We cannot let it protect us from living, under the guise of protecting us from dying.**

Now, let's pause to consider our worst fear: *What if you died in a terrorist attack or because of exposure to anthrax or smallpox?*

Please allow me to change the question from what is imagined to what is inevitable: *What if you died?*

We need to change the question from *what* to *when*. *When it is your time, will you be ready?*

I believe therein lies the key. We would answer that 'we are not really *afraid* to die; we are just not *ready* to die.'

Well, that leads us to the final two questions: *How do you make ready for something that does not announce its arrival? What constitutes being ready?*

I can tell you it is not the accumulation of things. It is not even the length of your days. It is knowing that you have lived your life with meaning. It is living life with purpose. Well, Jesus Christ gives both meaning and purpose to life, *and* to death.

That attitude of readiness dispels so much fear and births so much clarity. It goes far beyond preparing you to die; it gives you the courage to truly live: *"[I] will have sufficient courage so that now, as always, Christ will be exalted in my body, whether by life or by death. For to me, to live is Christ and to die is gain"* (Phil 1:20-21 NIV).

I am in no way advocating that we embrace an attitude toward death similar to that which the terrorists have. That attitude opens the door to spirits of suicide. I am saying, however, that having Jesus as the Lord of your life takes away the ability of our enemy to use the threat of death against us. How empowering it is to realize that we can't lose either way! So, even though life is uncertain, we can rest in the certainty of His Lordship.

"We are not our own bosses to live or die as we ourselves might choose. Living or dying we follow the Lord. Either way we are His. Christ died

and rose again for this very purpose, so that He can be our Lord both while we live and when we die" (Rom 14:7-9 TLB).

Unless we cast off the "spirit of fear", we will be afraid to truly live. Our creativity will be held captive, not by terrorists, but by terror that resides in our own mind. We will surrender our imagination in life to the dream of death – long before it even arrives. We will miss the joy of life, because we allowed fear to kill us long before we physically die.

This must be our affirmation, "**Because I choose to live, terrorists may kill my body, they will never take my life!"**

So, we will be free to dream, to live, to love, to laugh and to serve. And when 'our time' does come, we will be free to leave.

We will not give in to the destructive forging of fear and terror, for then we would die before we ever wake.

"OUR GREATEST ENEMIES ARE NOT
WILD BEASTS OR DEADLY GERMS
BUT FEARS THAT PARALYZE THOUGHT,
POISON THE MIND
AND DESTROY CHARACTER.
OUR ONLY PROTECTION AGAINST
FEAR IS FAITH."

- RYLLIS GOSLIN LYNIP

CHAPTER THREE

Fear Anti-Bodies

In just a matter of weeks, our once secure nation discovered, firsthand, the horrors of terrorism. Our enemies succeeded in hitting their intended targets because our psyche has been affected and our lives have been changed by fear.

Now we pause every time a plane flies overhead. Fear creeps into our homes through the images on the nightly news. It walks with us on our daily journey to the mailbox. It waits for any opportunity to attach itself to our souls.

We must now deal with invisible enemies who release invisible death into the air. We cannot ignore that the Bible refers to the spiritual force behind these acts as *"The Prince of the Power of the Air"* (Eph 2:2 NASU). In that verse it also states that his evil spirit *"is now working in the sons of disobedience"*. How true!

Demonic spirits are working in those who grow anthrax spores and expose innocent people to them. Demonic spirits were working in the suicide hijackers to drive them to those horrendous acts. Those demonic spirits can only be confronted and conquered by Spiritual warriors. That is why I am redundant in my call to the Church to step into its position in these critical times.

Because of the anthrax scare, our government and the pharmaceutical company that manufactures Ciprofloxacin have formally agreed to make certain that the demand for the antibiotic can be met. This medication, when introduced into the body, will attack and destroy the deadly, invisible disease caused by the anthrax bacterium.

As the nation clamors for this antibiotic, **the Church needs to release our own Spiritual anti-Bodies into the air to fight and destroy the deadly, unseen particles of fear that seem to be absorbed with our every breath in these**

uncertain times.

Antibiotics are *introduced into* the body, while antibodies are *produced in* the body to fend off invading substances.

Are you aware that the other name for the Church is *the Body of Christ*? Now is the time for *this* Body to produce anti-Bodies to defend against the deadly disease of fear and to assault the invisible, invading virus of terror.

When the Body of Christ produces the anti-Bodies, there will be a 'release' in the Spirit realm, not just to combat infectious fear and terror in the mind, but also to attack the evil Prince of the Power of the Air.

What are these cosmic anti-Bodies that are released in the Body of Christ's defense? What are these fear anti-Bodies? The answer is found in The Second Book of Kings, Chapter 6:

There was an occasion when an enemy king was hot after the Prophet Elisha. He dispatched an entire army for this one dangerous man. You see, Elisha had been prophesying the king's secret military agenda, preventing him from implementing his planned surprise attacks against the people of God.

The army came by night and surrounded the

city of Dothan, where the prophet lived. When the assistant to the prophet arose early that morning, he went outside to find their predicament somewhat precarious. He rushed in to tell the prophet, who, much to the assistant's dismay, was not the least bit disturbed by the news of the surrounding army. Elisha's response was, "Don't worry about it. There's nothing to be afraid of."

"Yeah," the assistant thought, "you didn't see what I saw."

To reassure the assistant, Elisha went on to tell him that, "We have more on our side than there are out there."

Well, that did not comfort the assistant, because no matter how he counted, he only came up with 'two' versus a whole army. Maybe there was even more reason to be worried, since Elisha didn't seem to realize the gravity of the situation.

There was a disparity in the attitude of the prophet and that of his assistant, which was based on how each of them viewed the same situation. It was resolved when Elisha prayed this interesting prayer: *"O LORD, open his eyes so he may see"* (vs. 17 NIV). It was not that the assistant was blind to the physical realm; he just could not see into the

Spiritual realm.

Suddenly, the Lord caused the assistant's eyes to be opened to what was transpiring in the heavenly sphere. To his astonishment, when his vision was enabled in that unseen realm, he saw a supernatural host. There stood fierce, superior, angelic warriors at the ready to fight on their behalf. That vision enabled him to overcome all of his fears.

The events of September 11th and thereafter have affected our vision. We have been blinded by pain, grief, rage, bitterness, revenge and loss of control. We have been blinded by what we see on the news. We have even been blinded by what we have imagined.

Now we are looking for antibiotics for fear of being exposed to a disease, when we should be looking for anti-Bodies because we have been exposed to the demonic!

As the Body of Christ, we should have a different perspective on the recent events. Accordingly, our response should be different. And because of our unique vision, we have a responsibility to open the eyes which have been blinded by the dense, gloomy cloud of what was once our wholeness.

We must cause eyes to be opened to see beyond the images on the news. We must see the real perpetrators and masterminds of the horrors – the infectious, demonic spiritual forces. Then, we must hold in everyone's view the mighty anti-Bodies standing at the ready, in the heavenly realm.

Just as fear skews perspective, faith rights vision. Therefore, we must draw our focus to the One Spiritual source with the power to destroy the spreading bacterium of fear, and the invisible particle of terror that are infecting the air. The Church must produce the much-needed anti-Bodies that will heal the wounds of our sorrow, grief and pain.

Thereafter, we must administer **the antidote for fear**!

"There is no fear in love; but ***perfect love casts out fear****, because fear involves torment. But he who fears has not been made perfect in love"* (1 John 4:18 NKJV).

An antidote is given to counteract a poison and render it harmless. The poison that fear releases is neutralized by *the perfect love of God*! (Understand, this does not refer to our love *for* God; it refers to God's love *for us*.)

Oh, that you could grasp *"the breadth and length and height and depth"* of God's love! (Eph 3:18). It transcends our ability to truly explain. His love provides a caring that gives a sense of safety and calm. His love *"casts out"* dread caused by the uncertainty of what the future may hold. It neutralizes the poison that produces fear in the mind. It counteracts terror that *"involves torment"*. His love ministers peace to the soul. The genuine experiencing of God's love will deliver you from the *"spirit of fear"*.

God's love for us is what motivated Him to send Jesus. At first, Jesus was His "only begotten Son" but, now God has more children — us! Me and you! He loved us so much that He adopted us as His own children.

My son, Barrington, is adopted. I tell Barrington the wonderful thing about being adopted is that *I chose him*! Think about it. God chose you! He loved you just that much!

When you begin to know how much He loves you and who you are in Him, it circumvents the *"spirit of fear"*. But, when you don't know who you are, the *"spirit of fear"* introduces the *"spirit of bondage"*.

"For you did not receive the spirit of bondage again to fear, but you received the Spirit of adoption by whom we cry out, 'Abba, Father'" (Rom 8:15 NKJV).

"Abba" means Daddy. You can call God "Daddy"! Then, knowing that you are His child and that He is your Daddy doesn't leave room for the those spirits of fear and bondage.

"For God has not given us a spirit of fear, but of power and of love and of a sound mind" (2 Tim 1:7 NKJV).

In this scripture, Paul reassures Timothy that the "spirit of fear" is not God-given and he affirms that love counteracts it. Then he adds two additional counter agents – *power* and *a sound mind.*

This "power" is more than an enabling ability; it is 'might'. Notice that to counter the *spirit* of fear we have the *spirit* of power. In other words, we have Spiritual might to overcome this unseen spirit enemy.

Next we have "a sound mind". Our mind is the place where fear would reside. God equips us with sound judgment and rationale thinking to counter the state of mind that terror brings and to overcome the imagination of fear. Simply put, the

Spirit of God enables us to bring our emotions under control.

So, the Church is uniquely prepared for this onslaught of this enemy. We are equipped internally for these foes who wage war inside the mind. Our ability to activate anti-Bodies, plus having the antidote ensures our success against the infectious enemy of terror. They empower us to stave off the invasion of fear.

We can be healed. We can be whole. We will be victorious!

"The LORD is my light and my salvation,
whom shall I fear?
The LORD is the strength of my life,
of whom shall I be afraid?
When evil men advance against me
to devour my flesh,
when my enemies and my foes attack me,
they will stumble and fall.
Though an army besiege me,
my heart will not fear;
though war break out against me,
even then will I be confident."

- Psalms 27:1-3 NIV

"The only sure way to take
the fear out of living
Is to keep a respectful fear
of God in our lives."
- Eugene Asa Carr

CHAPTER FOUR

Hijacked!

Some have asked the question concerning the horrors of September 11th, "Was this a judgment against America?" I cannot say that this was a judgment against our country, but I will say that this is an indictment against the American Christian Church!

The tragedy goes beyond four planes being hijacked, and the catastrophic sequence of events in the aftermath of those hijackings. It even goes beyond having our postal services hijacked and being used to make deadly deliveries. What is most tragic is the realization that the American Christian Church has been hijacked. Hijacking, simply put, means “to seize control, for the purpose of changing the course, destiny and purpose.” The enemy has definitely gotten the church off its course.

When I was growing up, there was a song that the old church mothers used to sing, which then seemed funny, but in retrospect was prophetic:

“Don’t let the devil ride...
Cause if you let him ride, he’ll try to drive...
If you let him drive, he’ll turn you around;
So don’t let him ride.”

It all started when the devil passed through our spiritual security checkpoints, not just because he blended into the church, but mostly because the church has blended into our postmodern society. We didn’t recognize him when he boarded with his own flight plans. He has succeeded in this hijacking, giving the church an alternate destination. Ever so slight deviations in the flight path have altered the course of the church’s destiny, preventing us from arriving at our purpose.

Instead of being worship centers, we have become entertainment centers. Instead of a life-changing Word, our sermons must appease the emotions. Instead of Spirit-filled ministry that convicts sinners, we offer generic services that do not offend the visitors and unsaved. Instead of representing the theocratic kingdom of heaven, we have become political, afraid of causing conflict with governing boards. Instead of being a relevant force in our changing world, we have become mired in tradition. Instead of being ministers of reconciliation, we have become ambassadors of condemnation.

What happened to the church being the Temple of the Lord? When did we stop being a place where lives were changed and turn into just another gathering place? When did we lose the ability to heal the broken heart? What happened to it being The Lord's House of Prayer for all nations? (Isaiah 56:7 and Mark 11:17)

I am even more disturbed at the revelation that this church hijacking, too, was carried out with spiritual box cutters. That's all our enemy had, because he had previously been stripped of any real weapons in his possession. Jesus took care of that at Calvary. Not only did Jesus disarm him, He also demoralized him. Our adversary was publicly defeated, then it was played back as a training film to show us how we are to triumph over him as well. Read Colossians 2:15.

Since Jesus disarmed him, the enemy has been reduced to using only makeshift weapons. However, they should not be effective. Regardless of what type of weapon *he* forms against you, it should not work! (Isaiah 54:17a)

Consider this: the weapons that the terrorists used against us on September 11th were not theirs, but ours. They hijacked our planes and turned them into guided missiles, to accomplish their evil plans. The only thing that they had of their own were their lives—and they were only able to use those once.

Without any real weapons, Peter refers to our adversary *"as a roaring lion"* (1 Pet 5:8 KJV). He is making a big noise, because his strength is not in his stealth or his spikes, but in his snarl, which spawns fear.

A fearful church allowed those hollow growls to effect this hijacking. Now the church has apparently been so stricken by terror that we have been scared to witness to the lost. We have been too timid to tell the unsaved about Jesus Christ. They are willing to lay down their lives for their cause, yet we are unwilling to be laughed at for the cause of our faith. We have been fearful of being ridiculed or humiliated for our cause, and they are not afraid to die for theirs. Their zeal disciplines them, yet we, who are called disciples, have no zeal for dread of being labeled "fanatical". They are not averse to 'fight' for their beliefs, but we are averse to 'confront' for ours. We have embraced embarrassment over enthusiasm. We have the Truth, yet we are reluctant to offend anyone with our faith. We are worried that our fervor might cost us a friend.

I wonder how many people died in the World Trade Center, in the Pentagon, and on those planes without knowing Jesus Christ, because some Christian was afraid to share the gospel with them?

We have been so anxious to advance in the system of the world, that we have not advanced the Kingdom of God. We have so wanted to be comfortable that we have become cowardly. Well, how comfortable are we now?

This was not just a wake up call for America. When that shrill alarm sounded, it was also a wake up call for the Church. The Bible is clear on what the Church should do when it receives a wake up call, such as the one received on September 11th. King Solomon gives us the divine plan for responding to alarming events: *"If Thy people be put to the worse before the enemy, because they have sinned against Thee; and shall return and confess Thy name, and pray and make supplication before Thee in this house"* (2 Chron 6:24-25a KJV).

America was certainly *"put to the worse"* on Tuesday, 9/11. But the scripture instructs us, in such an emergency, to make a 911 call — to heaven. 'If such horrors cause us to realize that we have been off course, and if we turn back to You, in an effort to get back on course, will You hear our prayers, and forgive us of our sins?'

God, Himself, gives us an assurance that He will respond to us when we seek Him - after we have been *"put to the worse"*. Then, because we have returned to our pursuit of Him, He adds the promise that He will heal our land: *"If my people, who are called by my name, will humble themselves, and pray, and seek my face, and turn from their wicked ways; then will I hear from heaven, and will forgive their sin, and heal their land."* (2 Chronicles 7:14 NKJV)

Can you see that the healing of our land rests with the spiritual activity of His people? The salvation of the nation will happen when "those who are called by [His] name" repent, or return to the right course and righteous purpose. The protection of this nation will be ensured when the Church is restored to its ordained position and functions in its God-ordained role. (More of the Church's critical role is defined in the pages ahead.)

The enemy made a gross miscalculation on Tuesday, September 11th. In his effort to use terror to control us, he awoke a sleeping giant – the Church. Now, we are casting off the restraints of fear and doubt, securing ourselves in the flight deck, reassuming control, and getting back to the Master's flight plan. And, when the church gets back on course, then our nation can get back on course.

Critical to our return to course is our recognition of the original flight plan and our original mission. Jesus, at His departure from this world, commanded and commissioned us to spread the Gospel (Matt 28:18-20; Mk 16:15-16; Acts 1:8). The enemy had taken more serious the carrying out of his commission than we had ours. He was more diligent in spreading his fear through the news and death through the mail than we had been in spreading the Good News of Abundant Life. He was more intent in commandeering *our* tools to use as weapons for *his* purpose; while the Church had been slow to use our own Spiritual weapons or to take advantage of the world's technology or even commandeer the enemy's tools. We must take seriously our charge and carry out our commission, *by any means necessary*.

We cannot hesitate. Timing is of the essence. We must act now! Our message is a very relevant. Our ministry is very needed. The Church is the key to victory in *our war against terror*.

At this point, I must give a caveat to the Church and its leadership: the Church must not let the government set its agenda or flight plan in this crucial season. As the government coordinates its multi-pronged attack on terrorism, its leaders acknowledge that the Church is critical to the success of the mission. They recognize the *religious* impact of this war, but they have not fully grasped the *Spiritual* impact. Out of their limited understanding, and with their own objectives in mind, they are encouraging Christian Church leaders to embrace leaders of the Muslim faith. The government wants to display the Church in that union to communicate the message to the world that this war is not America against Islam. If we allow the government's agenda to supercede our God agenda, this can be tantamount to allowing the Church to be hijacked again. This time by the government and our God-ordained destination will be changed, in accordance to *their* flight plan.

This is borne out by their inclusion of the Church in the war on terror abroad, but our exclusion from the matter of the bio-terror attacks here at home. When asked about the connection of the two, President Bush said that *"Both series of actions were motivated by evil."* They have not uncovered any evidence, to date, to link the terrorist attacks together in the natural, but our president has acknowledged the link in the spiritual. Both find their origin in the demonic. Then, who better to lead in the fight against this evil? Who better to send to the frontline than the Church?

So, invited or not, the Church must place itself in the center of both theatres of operations and lead in the fight against fear and terror. It is for the saving of our nation, our families and our future. And when we take up our position, this will be the Church's finest hour!

"THERE IS AMERICA, FULL OF FEAR
FROM ITS NORTH TO ITS SOUTH,
FROM ITS WEST TO ITS EAST.
THANK GOD FOR THAT."
- OSAMA BIN LADEN

"THE LORD IS ON MY SIDE;
I WILL NOT FEAR.
WHAT CAN MAN DO TO ME?"
- PSALMS 118:6 KJV

CHAPTER FIVE

Our Finest Hour!

It has been said that this is America's defining moment. I declare that this is the Church's defining moment, and it must be our finest hour. The Church has a unique role and responsibility in this strange season. We must have an "*understanding of the times to know what [we] ought to do*" (1 Chron 12:32 NKJV). So...

While President Bush leads our nation and the international community in this New War Against Terrorism, the Church must boldly step into its critical leadership role in this war. Our nation's Commander-in-Chief opened the door for us when he declared *"Ours is a war against evil"*, and that 'this war cannot be won using conventional tactics and conventional strategies alone'. Church leaders must step through that opening as competent warriors against evil. Then we must reveal the Spiritual strategies that transcend 'convention' and ensure a whole victory when this non-conventional war is completed.

The War Council has named this military operation "Enduring Freedom". Our *liberties* may be secured by the might of our military, but our f*reedom* can only endure when it is secured in our souls and in our spirits.

The President may lead the fight for freedom and to vanquish terrorism from our soil, but only the Church can lead in the fight for enduring freedom from fear, and to vanquish terror from our soul.

While our military responses are governed by 'rules of convention' and center around the policy of "minimal loss of life", only the Church can match the enemy's level of violence and aggression. Jesus prepares us for this class of warfare with this directive: *"the Kingdom of*

Heaven suffers violence, and the violent take it by force" (Matt 11:12 NKJV). We must be offensive with the weapon of the Word. We must be violent in our intercession. We must be militant in our worship. We must be fanatical in our witnessing.

America's military fights according to rules while our enemies adhere to none. In the tactical strikes by the U.S. armed forces, their objective is to accomplish their mission with a minimum number of losses and casualties. Our enemies carry out their missions at any cost, including the cost of their own lives. However, as a nation, we don't like war to be ugly.

The Church's Field Manual sends the Spiritual soldier in for "violent" warfare. It gives clear orders to 'totally destroy the enemy' and not to apologize for the casualties.

The Church's objective must be to fight until the enemy is completely defeated. Then, in victory we must not become humane to our defeated foes. We cannot give them provisions to rebuild. We must not retreat from the ground we have gained. As Spiritual warriors we will recover everything that the enemy stole from us, plus collect all of his spoils as our trophies!

While the State Department uses shuttle diplomacy to build and maintain coalitions among our allies, Church leaders should be building prayer coalitions that cross denominational and racial boundaries, to secure this victory. Just as the twelve tribes of Israel formed one strong nation, our many denominations make up the One Church. Now, the One Church must truly represent "United We Stand". We must beseech God for our homeland and our homes, as one voice, because His movement is based on our prayers.

It is not enough that we pray for those victimized by the horrible attacks or that we intercede for our leaders to have wisdom in this time of 'life and death' decision making (Prov 20:18). We must do more than pray for those who have worked in and around the damage, and for those who have been put out of work because of the damage. The Church's imperative is raise its prayer banner, stained with the blood of Jesus, and aggressively engage in prayer strategies that drive back and overthrow the powers of darkness.

While the military calls up reservists and dispatches troops, the Church must call up spiritual warriors and dispatch intercessors across this nation. This is not a religious war, but it is a Spiritual war against demon spirits of terrorism, whether they cloak themselves in robes of Islam or the Ku Klux Klan. We are fighting more than Osama bin Laden's terrorist plan; we are fighting Satan's plan to rule by terror and fear.

The Church must send in our superior ground troops, on their knees — in prayer and intercession. We must provide air cover with praise and worship. As our military is responding with force, our Spiritual soldiers must carry out persistent Spiritual assaults against the forces of evil.

U.S. military might includes the Special Operative Forces: the Green Beret, Delta Force and Navy SEALs. Well, the Church provides the *'Counter-Terrorism Special Spiritual Ops'* in this war. These Spiritual Ops must aggressively defend against the dark forces that would destroy our inner solace and drive us to hide in the caves of life.

While the intelligence community is gathering information to locate terrorist cells, our federal law enforcement officials are working to identify and track down the

invisible bio-enemies. However, at this writing, our military has not been able to specifically locate our main terrorist target abroad, and federal authorities have been stumped here on the homeland, as the try to track the sources of the bio-terror attacks. They have no idea who or what they are looking for.

That has been the trademark of this war – our enemies on both fronts remain invisible. Any strategist will tell you that the most important rule of war is "know your enemy".

Well, the Church already has intelligence on the enemy. We know who the real enemy is: it is our adversary, the devil, the prince of the power of the air. He is still seeking to bring chaos and unrest into the world in his effort to secure his place as despot through fear, terror and oppression.

Not only does the Church know the enemy, we also have special insight into his demonic "wiles". Our battlefield advantage is that since we *"are not unaware of his schemes",* Satan cannot *"outwit us"* (2 Cor 2:11 NIV).

Because we are not just fighting terrorism, but combating terror, the Church has another clear advantage: *"For God has not given us a spirit of fear"* (2 Tim 1:7 NKJV). The Church is girded by the Spirit, experienced and combat ready to counter demonic activity and overcome the assault of fear.

While "America Strikes Back" with warships, planes, bombs and troops — to attack and root out *terrorists*, it is the Church that must fight to root out *terror.* Terrorism has found its way to our shores and terror now resides in the hearts of so many. The Church must be aggressive in our mission to *restore the souls* that have been victimized.

The Bible clearly speaks to the battle in the realm where terror would entrench itself. *"Our struggle is not against flesh and blood, but against rulers, against authorities, against the powers of this dark world, against spiritual forces of evil in the heavenly realm"* (Eph 6:12 NIV).

This is the heart of the message of this book: This war transcends the flesh realm. It is against wickedness. We are battling dark forces of evil. It may sound like Star Wars, but this is not a movie. Yes, it is a cosmic battle, but it is only through the fight in this realm that we will defeat the forces behind airplane hijackings and airmail anthrax attacks. Only the Church is combat-ready to defeat the enemy in this realm.

The world is now focused on Osama bin Laden, his highly structured Al Qaeda organization and its invisible network of terror. Evidence points to him as being behind the terror that has shaken our nation.

Bin Laden, as the director, has proclaimed himself as the "emir" or prince. Those in authority next to him include Muhammad Atef and Ayman al-Zawahiri. They are responsible for operations and supposedly handled certain aspects of the September 11th attack. Al Quaeda is a highly structured global network with cells in over 60 countries. They supposedly have hundreds of invisible "sleeper agents" hiding among us, waiting to be "awakened".

The Church's Field Manual has already made us aware of the one responsible for the terror, giving us elaborate detail regarding the structure of his invisible network of terror. We have clear 'intel' on the levels of demonic authority and activity that we must contend with. First, there are the ruling demonic princes or 'emirs', followed by demonic jurisdictional authorities. Next there are the rulers of dark terror cells, then a huge number of evil spirits awaiting their assignments. (Eph 6:12) With this intelligence, the Church is further prepared to deal with this demonic order.

Additionally, we are instructed that, *"though we live in the world, we do not wage war as the world does. The weapons we fight with are not the weapons of the world. On the contrary, they have divine power to demolish strongholds... and we take captive every thought to make it obedient to Christ"* (2 Cor 10:3-4 NIV).

There are several things we need to notice in this scripture: First, we are called to target and destroy the enemy's stronghold, his fortress, his place of security and planning. That transcends the caves of the Al Qaeda or the lethal anthrax laboratories of the bio-terrorists. It is attacking the spiritual fortresses that the enemy would establish in the mind and in the imagination. We must ascend on and demolish his stronghold of fear.

That is why, secondly, we are directed to fight in the theatre of the mind. That is where the spores of fear are released. That is where the bombs of terror are dropped. It must be *there* that we carry out our sortie against the unseen, internal enemy.

To accomplish those objectives, thirdly, we have been outfitted with special weapons. Unlike those of a conventional army, our weapons are Spiritual, they are invisible, and most importantly, they have an awesome divine power to fight and defeat the invisible foe.

Our most important weapon is the Word of God. Most efficient of our armament, it has the ability to engage the invisible enemy on the open battlefield and covertly. The Word of God can root out the unseen enemy that has hidden in the crevices between our soul and spirit, wounding our inner being (Heb 4:12). It can penetrate our self-defenses put up by emotions and address the real issues that hold our heart captive.

It is the necessary weapon for driving out the "spirit of fear". It guides us in dealing with the terror that would overload our senses. It teaches us how to counter the things that would steal our inner peace. The weapon of the Word brings our whole system back into balance.

In times of nervousness, it tells you what to think on (Phil 4:7). It helps you in dealing with anxiety (Phil 4:6). When fear creep in, it helps you guard your mind (Is 41:10-13). This doesn't even scratch the surface of the ability of the Word to guard our hearts and mind, reassuring us in times of uncertainty.

Fourthly, alongside our arms, we have been uniformed with special armor to protect us against the weapons of the invisible enemy. Warfare in the Spirit realm requires Spiritual armor worn by a Spiritual people. (Eph 6:13-17)

One of the most critical pieces of our armor against fear is "the helmet of salvation". It covers the most important part of your being in this war on terror – your mind.

Have you noticed in almost any kind of combat, whether it be in military or sport, head protection is consistent and consistently hard! That's because a blow to the head affects the entire body. It can disable you, render you unconscious or even kill you. Well, that's the end-game of fear. It doesn't care which one of those it causes to happen to you; it's just aiming to strike a blow to your mind.

Having the helmet of salvation protects you from the wounds the enemy would inflict on your head – the fear he would lodge there, the anxiety that would disable you, the terror that would render you senseless, then leave your being disabled or paralyzed.

The helmet of salvation is the *crown* of our salvation. Not having *"it"* makes us vulnerable to the enemy. The *"it"* is more than the helmet. The *"it"* is salvation. If you don't have salvation that comes through faith in Jesus Christ, then you stand on the battlefield unprotected. And this is not a time to live in the world unprotected! Receive God's free gift of salvation. Armour up!

Finally and even more important than what we wear is what's on the inside of us. We are to be "filled" with *His* Spirit. This enables us to go into battle with the surety that *"greater is He who is in you than he who is in the world"* (1 John 4:4 NASU). We are internally empowered for the fight.

While thousands are lining up to receive anti-biotic treatments as a guard against anthrax, the Church has been uniquely equipped to deal with the enemy's demonic poisons. Being Spirit-filled is like being inoculated against many of the devil's weapons. Jesus described this unique protection: *"They will take up serpents; and if they drink anything deadly, it will by no means hurt them"* (Mark 16:18a NKJV). I am not saying that a Spirit-filled believer cannot be touched by anthrax, small-pox or any other forms of bio-terror, but I am saying that there is no greater anti-Body than the Holy Spirit in the body!

What an advantage we have, both over the natural realm and our demonic enemy!

Our government recently created the office of Homeland Security and appointed a Secretary to that post, to establish new internal security measures. Before September 11th, we felt safe from enemies abroad and certain that there were no real threats at home. Now, the things that were once commonplace in our everyday lives, like airplanes and airmail, cause trepidation. What was once normal, now makes us nervous. In this day of 'weapons grade' aerosol anthrax, we have lost what it means to simply "breathe easy".

Those who are responsible for our security have become consumed with their own, as they, themselves, have become targets of bio-terror. Now, the Center for Disease Control has issued a warning to the entire nation to be on alert. Health care officials have been told to remain on 24-hour guard for the intentional release of biological agents.

Our real security will only be ensured when the Church takes up its position and 'stands guard' in the Spirit realm. The Church is equipped with a special armament to deflect external and internal assault of terror. We have been issued a *"shield of faith"*. It has been given to us so that we can raise it as a defense against the *"flaming arrows of the evil one"*, whether those arrows be veiled in planes or postal packages (Eph 6:16 NIV).

Faith is the most powerful force against fear. The Church is well able to beat back that invisible enemy, would we just raise our *"shield <u>of faith</u>"* and *"fight the good fight <u>of faith</u>"* (1 Tim 6:12 KJV).

We must bring to naught demonic strategies of fear, terror, anxiety, depression and panic. We must bind terrorist spirits of mass murder, genocide, suicide, hatred, division and deception. We must shine the Light on those evil spirits that thrive in darkness. That is the reason Jesus gave the Church Spiritual power and authority!

While Congress has passed sweeping anti-terrorism legislation to provide our law enforcement agencies with requested tools for our homeland defense, the Church must specifically enact counter-terror measures to guard the hearts and minds of our children and families. We must administer the "Peace of God", so that our nation and our communities do not succumb to panic, uncertainty, nervousness and depression.

Our responsibility is to prevent any downward spiral from anxiety to anger and from hurt to hatred. We must also guard against the effects that the constant exposure to reports of terrorism have on our psyche and on our hope.

Churches have the greatest capacity, just by our combined numbers, to address our national condition and comfort our wounded souls. We also have the greatest capacity for the individual touch that is necessary to minister security in this time of heightened insecurity. The Church must provide the ministry that moves us from brokenness to wholeness and from pain to promise.

As everything has shifted in response to the world that changed on September 11th, the Church must make the necessary "leader-shift" into our position and purpose in this decisive day. In so doing, this will be the Church's finest hour!

*"If your knees knock,
kneel on them."*

On a sign posted outside a church
in London During World War II
when that city was being bombed
almost daily by Nazi warplanes

CHAPTER SIX

September 12th

Even though terrorists executed a portion of their plan on September 11th, God has already taken their evil deeds and turned the results for good for *"the saving of many lives"* (Gen 50:20 NIV).

As many as 5,000 people died on September 11th, most of them buried in the rubble of Ground Zero, unlikely to be physically recovered. Those lives have become Spiritual seed, sown into Spiritual ground for the redemption of 5,000 times 5,000 souls for the Kingdom of God.

The enemy's plan was to destroy key buildings, and leave certain parts of our culture in ruin. Instead, he has given us *"burnt stones"* which *can be used* to build to the glory of God. (Nehemiah 4:1-5)

Before September 11th, we were still debating the issue of prayer in school. After September 11th, there was hardly a school in our nation where someone was not praying. In the days following September 11th, there were more people in prayer services and vigils than probably ever before in the history of our nation. Our enemy didn't count on that.

Until September 11th, Satan had just about succeeded in shutting God out of the classroom. Until September 11th, he had just about succeeded in stopping the government from making references to God. Until September 11th, he had just about removed any references to Christianity from all public buildings. Until September 11th, he had just about succeeded in even X-ing Christ out of Christmas.

After September 11th, our president is quoting scripture. After September 11th, our elected officials are making their presence known at prayer meetings. After September 11th our entertainment community takes a lead in a nationally televised prayer service. There was a time when it would have only been called a memorial service. Now they are not ashamed to call it a prayer service. After September 11th, you can't go anywhere in our nation and not see a sign that says "In God We Trust", or "God Bless America", or "Pray for Our Nation".

Have you noticed how quiet the atheists have been? Have you noticed how quiet those who fight against our prayer liberties have been? Their quietness is explained in the expression, "There are no atheists in foxholes". They realize that they need somebody bigger than themselves to trust, and it is only in God that we can trust.

The Church was given a fresh opportunity after September 11th to preach to a world that is now ready to listen. When those towers fell, the fallow ground of millions of hearts was broken up, softened to receive the seed of the Word. We must seize this moment!

What happened to us on that terrible Tuesday affected the soul of America, and only the Church is equipped to deal with the 'soul destroyers' and minister healing to the soul.

Even in the ugly face of the bio-terror attacks since September 11th, there are opportunities for the Church to take what was meant for evil and turn it for good to *"the saving of many lives"*. We are the ones with the ability to minister the "Breath of Life" in this time of inhalation anthrax. The world is ready for our message of *"abundant life"* in this time when the enemy delivers packages of death.

So the call goes out to my brothers and sisters who stand behind the podium every "Lord's Day" to give a life-changing Word. We must position ourselves as commanders in this war, raising up an army of saints to stage a vicious counterassault against the dark forces that would seize our souls. Wielding the awesome weapon of the Word of God and fortified with the tactical tools of courage and hope, we must lead our warriors into battle. We must fight fear, trounce terror, subdue sorrow, defeat depression and triumph over torment.

Along with our offensive posture, we must defend the delicate soil of our hearts and minds. For the enemy would contaminate us with bitterness and hatred. He would contain us with uncertainty and doubt. He would condemn us to a future without promise. We cannot let his plan come to pass.

The Church must lead in the recovery process of our hearts from the ashes of fear and grief, then to the altars of faith and glory.

We must also shine as beacons of light, illuminating the way in a post-September 11th world, for fear resides in darkness. It is the Light that overcomes the darkness.

The Church has the critical message that the nation so desperately needs in this hour. And it is this message that will move our nation from being victims on September 11th to the process of being victors, beginning September 12th and every day thereafter!

The Church also has the critical ministry that will ensure that when the war has been completed, we will be more than safe; we will be healed and we will be whole.

Jesus, knowing that He was about to be murdered by terrorists, prepared His followers to not only survive, but also thrive in their own 'post-September 11th world':

"I am leaving you with a gift -
peace of mind and heart!
And the peace I give isn't fragile
Like the peace the world gives.
So don't be troubled or afraid.
I have told you all this so that
you will have peace of heart and mind.
Here on earth you will have
many trials and sorrows;
but cheer up,

for I have overcome the world."
(John 14:27 16:33 TLB)

Allow me, at this juncture, to say that I am not supposing to disqualifying psychology and medicine from their role in helping us to recover in this crisis and, in general, to help the individual to overcome fears and phobias. Those systems have great value. I do believe, however, that there are some things that the Church possesses that better qualifies us for this task.

Our theology gives us an answer to evil and a means to deal with it outside of ourselves. That is not to absolve the individual of personal responsibility. If anything, our theology makes the individual more responsible and more accountable.

We don't expect the individual to do it alone. Vital to our method is our *community of caring*, with love being the critical element.

We also have additional weapons for fighting fear: spiritual weapons not used in secular therapy.

The Church also does more than fight to keep fear from overcoming the individual. We fight to overcome fear at its source!

Kenneth C. Hauck, a trained psychologist

and author of *Christian Caregiving—a Way of Life** says *"I believe each of these systems has a unique and valuable contribution to make. Nevertheless, these approaches appear quite superficial when compared to the unique Christian perspective.*

Christian caregiving has significant advantages over any other method. The primary advantage is depth.

Of course, the techniques and perspective of psychology can be helpful. However, the best content and framework on which to build is the Christian one. I also believe that psychology needs theology to realize its greatest potential.

Psychology, sociology, and medicine cannot give the entire answer to the human condition. There is a significant gap left for theology."

The Church must not be reticent in our response. We must not be intimidated by the size of the horrors. We must not feel inferior to our secular counterparts. We must not turn away for the responsibilities that September 11th require us to shoulder. We are uniquely equipped for the task. For we know who holds all of our tomorrows.

*Kenneth C. Hauck, *Christian Caregiving—a Way of Life* (Minneapolis, MN, Augsburg Publishing House, 1984) 45-49

YOU SHALL NOT BE AFRAID
OF THE TERROR BY NIGHT,
NOR OF THE ARROW
THAT FLIES BY DAY"
- PSALMS 91:5 NKJV

CHAPTER SEVEN

Who's Scared Now?!

Daily the media is reporting to us how enemies of our *Shalom*, or peace, are successfully carrying out their plans to saturate our nation with fear and trembling.

The alleged mastermind of the hijacking atrocities, Osama bin Laden, has promised even more terror: *"I swear by God, who has elevated the skies without pillars, neither America nor the people who live in it will dream of security."*

Now, as our once certain peace seems precarious, we brace for future terrorist attacks and bio-terror exposures, as our government issues security alerts and health warnings.

President Bush, in his address to Congress after the first strikes on Afghanistan, stated that this would be "a lengthy campaign unlike any other we have ever seen." A United States Congressman told me personally that, while our military is in pursuit of terrorists, "There is very little we can do to *prevent* terrorism."

We must move wisely in the exercise of our military options because there is the dreaded potential of exacerbating the terrorism problem. In our effort to mute Osama bin Laden, we could actually multiply him, by making him a martyr to extremist Islamic fundamentalist. The Taliban has already promised that if anything happens to bin Laden, they will produce "hundreds of other Osamas". The President of Pakistan, Pervez Musharraf, said that 'getting bin Laden and the Al Qaeda network is like getting only a branch on the tree of terrorism. We are still nowhere near the root.'

Then, there is much evidence that links Iraq to both the planning of the terrorist assaults and supplying the weapons-grade anthrax which has been released in our country. Saddam Hussein seems to be, once again, in our military scopes.

It is apparent that the fighting won't end in

Afghanistan. In preparation for the expansion of the war, the U.S. has already given the United Nations notice that we reserve the right to target other countries. So, as you are reading this, we have probably enlarged the scope of the fight.

We cannot be driven by sheer revenge, because to kill or capture one man won't satisfy our blood-thirst for the lives of our 5,000. Gandhi reminded us that a policy of "an eye for an eye only makes the whole world blind". Our purposes must rise above hatred and malevolence.

While our military is active abroad, our fears broaden at home as the threat of terror has graduated from bombs to bacteria. At first the enemy learned to become invisible in our culture. Then he learned to take the things of our culture and turn them against us. Things we never expected. Things we were never prepared for.

Never suspecting, our mail carriers became carriers of lethal letters, that have "killed the messengers" and spread death into the air. Bioterrorism has become a shocking reality to us, as our vocabulary has been expanded with words like "weapons-grade", and "aerosol" is now an adjective to anthrax and not just to our household air freshner.

As important as the news is to us, at times it only cultivates our growing insecurity and uncertainty. The media has informed us of the threat of smallpox and how unprepared the Center for Disease Control is to deal with exposure of the masses.

Terrorists have made things as ordinary traveling and opening the mail, or as necessary as breathing, dangerous. Next, we are warned, they may begin to target our food supply. Let's be honest, that makes it difficult *not* to be afraid.

We won't be able to "breathe easy" until the terrorists, who kill for the price of a stamp, are brought to justice. We won't feel safe in our skies again until we are confident that those who kill for the price of an airline ticket are no longer allowed on board.

We are already discussing future horrors. Analysts are talking about the threat of truck bombs, while some wonder will they go as far as the lone suicide bombers in Israel who show up in the mall or on buses with explosives attached to their bodies. And what about them flying a plane into a nuclear power plant?

Since mail is now being irradiated, the bio-terrorists have been thwarted in using the postal system to spread death. So, will they try to slip some bio-germ into the ventilation system of a government or office building?

We try not to even think about the weapons of mass destruction that are available on the black market since the breakup of the Soviet Union.

Too many threats! What is next? Where will it end, we wonder.

America has become besieged, not by foreign forces, but by fear. Simply put, as a people, we are scared. It is very clear that the enemies strategically targeted our minds when they attacked our nation. So, even when we win the fight with missiles and technology, unless we make advances on the battleground of the mind, we can't declare victory.

That is why the full participation of the Church is so critical in this war. We have a strategic role in both launching assaults on the enemy and defending the territory of the soul.

And when the Church, as a mighty Spiritual army, carries out its assignments, God will take the demonic strategies of fear and terror, and reverse them back on the en-

emy. Deuteronomy 2:25 describes what will happen: *"This day I will begin to put the dread and fear of you upon the peoples everywhere under the heavens, who, when they hear the report of you, shall tremble and be in anguish because of you"* (NASU).

That is a complete turnaround from where we started in Jeremiah, when hearing the report of the horrors caused anxiety to grip us, and sorrow to overwhelm us. When the activated Church stands up in this hour, in this defining moment, and takes our place of leadership and authority, the situation will reverse. Our Spiritual assault on the enemy will create the fear and dread of the Power mightier than the force of man!

It wouldn't be the first time that happened. There are several times, recorded in the scriptures, when fear circled back on the enemy, causing their defeat. One time, recorded in Second Kings, Chapter 7, an enemy had come against the army of God. Before they could attack, the enemy heard the sound of an advancing force. They knew for sure that the people of God had made an alliance with another army and that they were about to be overwhelmed by a joint military campaign. They knew they had no chance at victory. So, at that sound, they retreated in certain terror and with such haste that they left all of their weapons and supplies.

There was no advancing army (in the natural realm). The people of God had not joined forces with another military (on earth). There were no battalions breathing down on them (at least none they could see). God had simply caused them to hear "a noise" that put them to fear and to flight. That "noise" was the sound of Spiritual activity.

Spiritual movement is more powerful than the advance of any army. While it is beyond the 'tangible' realm, it is still very real. Movement in the Spirit realm happens when the Church is activated.

On another occasion there were three armies that made an alliance to join forces to attack King Jehoshaphat and the nation of Judah. In the face of that situation, the first thing the king did was the same thing President Bush did in the situation on September 11th — he called the nation to prayer.

As a result of seeking divine help through prayer, God gave them a war strategy. However, before they could 'fall in' for battle, He first gave them a directive regarding their attitude: *"Do not fear or be dismayed because of [them]"* (vs. 15). It will take a fearless army to defeat the "spirit of fear".

Then he gave them a very specific plan of attack. King Jehoshaphat, the commander-in-chief, was not to deploy the marines first. He was to send the Special Ops in first, the ones with first strike capabilities. He was to put the worshipers on the frontline! Yes, even in advance of the military. You see, it was 'a Spiritual thing'. (2 Chronicles 20)

What would be accomplished by positioning the worshipers first? Beyond it being an acknowledgment of the Spiritual nature of the conflict, it caused God to get personally involved. And it was His involvement that determined the outcome of the battle.

Our present conflict is also 'a Spiritual thing'. In this battle, too, it is the proper placement of the Spiritual warriors that will determine the outcome of the battle.

There was something remarkable that happened when the worshipers went first. As they began to engage in Spiritual warfare, *"The LORD set ambushes against the men"* (vs. 22 NIV). Their Spiritual activity activated God.

I don't know what the ambushes were that God set, but they caused the three armies to fight amongst themselves. They fought until they *"utterly killed.. one another"* (vs. 23 NKJV). The only thing God's people had to do after that was collect the victory spoils from a battle that they didn't even have to fight *in the natural realm.*

You know by now that the terrorist network is made up of various cells scattered throughout the world. I have no doubt that if the Church would boldly take a 'forward position' and war in the Spirit realm, God can "set ambushes" against them. We could suddenly see conflict rise among the various cells. That could lead to in-fighting. Whatever the dynamics would be thereafter, the end result could be that they destroy each other. They might expose one another's positions, tip officials off to strategic plans, reveal an operative's location or their weapons may activate on them before they can be used against anyone else. Any number of scenarios could actualize. Our enemies would be "ambushed" or "discomfited". All because we, the Church, positioned ourselves to fight in this battle. Then, who'll be scared?

(See the next chapter for a Spiritual strategy against bio-terrorism.)

It is important for us to also note, in the

aforementioned account, *how* the people prayed. First they acknowledged their fears. They admitted to God that they were afraid of the impending dangers. Next, they repented, confessing to their disobedience and neglect of God. Thirdly, they recognized God, honoring Him as being their keeper and their protection. Thereafter they asked God for help, for they knew they couldn't overcome their enemies on their own.

That should be our pattern for prayer as we deal with our invisible enemy. Yes, we should pray for the victims, their families, the relief workers, government officials and our military. But we must not feel that it is selfish to acknowledge our *own* fears and uncertainties in this time of national concern for others.

He wants us to come to Him, just like a child rushes to their parent when he or she is scared. We can tell Him that we are afraid of the uncertain dark. We can ask Him to look in the corners for the monsters that disturb our rest. We can admit to Him that we are having nightmares from the horrors we watched on the TV news. We can confess that our imagination has fed our fears.

"Cast all your anxiety on Him because He

cares for you" (1 Peter 5:7 NIV).

He is our Daddy! (Gal 4:6) He loves us dearly and it matters to Him what scares us. He doesn't want us living in the shadows. He doesn't want us to be harassed by fear and tormented by terror. He longs for us to crawl into the safety of His loving arms, so that He can hold us, kiss us and comfort us in His care.

Then, as those horrors have humbled us, we must move to repentance in our prayer. Repent for neglecting God until we are faced with difficulty. Don't worry, He's not holding it against you. (2 Cor 5:19; 1 John 1:9) You're already forgiven. He just doesn't like you making a habit of it!

Since 'repent' means 'to turn', it also involves making *the decision* to live life differently. (Many things of the Spirit begin with our own decisions.) It is in our repentance that we must decide to turn from fear and turn out anxiety. We must make the decision to no longer allow terror to take up residence in our soul. We must *choose* life.

The third part of the prayer is to recognize God. Even though this is directed *to Him*, it is specifically *for us*. Our acknowledgement of Him is not to "butter Him up" so that we can get Him to move in our favor. The significance of this is to make *our own soul*, the place where fear would reside, affirm that God is greater than what we fear and that He is also greater than our fears. It is to reassure our inner person that God is faithful. It is to restore the confidence that may have been shattered by our experiences.

"Yet there is one ray of hope: His compassion never ends. It is only the Lord's mercies that have kept us from complete destruction. Great is His faithfulness; His loving-kindness begins afresh each day. My soul claims the Lord as my inheritance; therefore I will hope in Him. The Lord is wonderfully good to those who wait for Him, to those who seek for him. It is good both to hope and wait quietly for the salvation of the Lord." (Lamentations 3:21-26 TLB)

Finally, we are to ask God for our specific warfare plan in this battle against fear and terror. He *will* give us a Spiritual strategy. Whether it be sending the worshipers first, or having prayer intercessors launch Spiritual smart bombs; He will give us a plan to "ambush" and "discomfit" the enemy.

"The Philistines returned and again spread out across the valley of Rephaim. When David

asked the Lord what to do, he replied, "Don't make a frontal attack. Go behind them and come out by the balsam trees. When you hear a sound like marching feet in the tops of the balsam trees, attack! For it will signify that the Lord has prepared the way for you and will destroy them." So David did as the Lord had instructed him and destroyed the Philistines all the way from Geba to Gezer." (2 Sam 5:22-25 TLB)

Do you see that? The Lord has prepared the way before us! So we must advance! We cannot be passive. We cannot allow Spiritual warfare to be treated as inconsequential. Prayer is not powerless! Intercession is not impotent! Praise and worship are not puny! The weapon of the Word is not weak! They are all potent spiritual weapons. They activate the Cosmic forces on our behalf. They have stopped the advance of many an enemy. They can "put 10,000 to flight." Against this invisible enemy, there is nothing more powerful than our unseen weapons.

Even now, the devil trembles at the thought that the Church would arise in this hour and engage him through the weapons and strategies given to us in the Word. *It scares him!*

"They that worship God
Merely from fear
Would worship the devil, too
If he appear"

- ANONYMOUS

CHAPTER EIGHT

Cracking Their Skulls

One of the most impressive things to me about the Bible is that this ancient book has the ability to speak to whatever situation I face today. I believe that is why it is called a "living book".

Do you know that in the Bible there is an account of a terrorist attacking and destroying a tower, killing over a thousand people? (Judges 9) We may not feel like we need to read that account since we just lived our own. But, did you know that the Bible speaks to how we can defeat the terrorists?

Now do I have your attention?

Abimelech bin Jerubbaal was his name. He came from a wealthy family. His father had been the governor of the region where he grew up. Abimelech, consumed by his ambition, resorted to terror to establish himself as governor after his father's death. His first terrorist act was to have 69 of his brothers and sisters killed, to rid himself of any rivalries, thereby securing his position. (He would have killed all 70 of them, but one brother managed to escape.)

Then he proceeded to eliminate those who did not adhere to *his* values and principles. With his band of terrorists, he attacked the city of Shechem. Shechem was a major city in their province.

People cowered in fear because of this terrible man. His ruthlessness had become legendary after murdering his own family. It was obvious that there were no limits to where this man would go to satisfy his selfish desires.

Abimelech attacked and burned a tower in Shechem, killing over a thousand men and women, leaving them and the building in ashes.

After succeeding in overcoming Shechem and exacting the intended horror in the first attack, he set his sights on Tower Two in the city of Thebez.

The Bible tells us that he then 'besieged' Thebez. That's a word that is descriptive of an interesting battle strategy. It involves first setting up camp around the city that is targeted for attack. The strategy in 'besieging' a city is to 'weaken it for the kill'

In those days, cities had walls around them for protection. If an enemy camped outside of those walls long enough, what once protected the city now only 'contained' it. Eventually all of the resources inside of the city would begin to be used up. Without the ability to leave for necessary replenishment, the depleted city would become vulnerable and acquiescent. (Is this not what fear does to our soul?)

The most critical part of besieging a city was to humiliate it. The army outside the gate would hurl, not stones or flaming arrows but 'threats' into the city. They would boast about their last victory. They would taunt with stories about the pain they inflicted on their last victims. They would brag on the strength and cruelty of their weapons. They made threats about their future violence. They would make promises not to leave anyone alive. This was done to demoralize the victims, causing fear to take root in their souls.

If they could defeat them with terror, then the physical battle would be an easy one.

After besieging Thebez, paralyzing them with

fear and tormenting them with terror, Abimelech made his move against the city.

As he approached Tower Two to set it ablaze and kill all of its occupants, something extraordinary happened: a woman dropped a stone from the window. (More precisely, it was the top portion of a millstone.) She aimed and released the stone so that it fell directly on the head of Abimelech, crushing his skull.

Mortally wounded, Abimelech called for his armorbearer. (They are like military caddies, carrying the warrior's weapons.) With his last breath, he quickly instructed hisarmorbearer to take his sword and run him through. In recognizing that he was dying, the most important thing to him as a warrior was that his epitaph would not read "a woman killed him" (Judges 9:54).

The armorbearer obeyed him and struck the *final blow* that took the life of Abimelech, but we all know that it was the woman who struck the *fatal blow.*

With the demise of terrorist Abimelech bin Jerubbaal, life returned to normal for the people of that province.

More than just paralleling the terrorist attack on our two towers in New York, there are some lessons to learn and some strategies to apply to *"crush the skull"* of our enemy. Very specifically, this scripture reveals the role of the Church in our efforts against bio-terrorism.

First, I must tell you who the characters represent: Abimelech, of course, is the Terrorist.

The Woman who dropped the stone, crushing the skull of the terrorist, is the Church. The Church is referred to as *a woman* throughout the scriptures, and notably regarded as *the Bride of Christ.* (Eph 5:25-32) Before I explain how the stone is dropped...

The Armorbearer represents the military and federal law enforcement officials. Notice in our story that the terrorist was fatally wounded by the woman, but ultimately killed by the armorbearer. The military abroad and our government at home will be able to strike the final blow against the terrorist if *the Lord's woman* would act quickly. The guardians of our land would be much more efficient and expeditious in their assignments against those who terrorize us, when the Church "drops the stone" to crush the head of our enemy.

When that woman acted, dropping that stone from that tower, she was not doing what she did for glory, attention or credit. She was doing it to save her life and the lives of her family. In the end, she didn't care who was recognized for stopping Abimelech, as long as he was stopped.

That's the way it will be with the Church. Our names will not be announced for our Cosmic warfare. We won't receive any medals for our Spiritual efforts. Not many people outside of the Church will even know we played any significant role. We don't care. (We'll get our recognition in the future.)

We *want* the military to stop Osama bin Laden. We *want* the FBI to capture the bio-terrorists. We *want* the CIA to disband Al Qaeda. We just realize that they will be swiftly successful if we, the Church, do our part promptly and passionately.

Church, we must drop the stone! What is the stone? It is a specific prayer strategy that God has given us to crush the head of the enemy.

Do you realize how accurate the woman had to be in dropping the stone? That's how precise our prayers must be. Yes, we have been praying, but our prayers have been gentle prayers of comfort and encouragement. We have been praying *for...* We must take aim and release the deadly stone of prayer *against...*

Just as with any military assault, our prayers must be executed with precision, targeting the enemy.

Our federal investigators and postal inspectors are faced with the difficult task of tracking down the sources of the bio-terror. They are urgently searching for clues to discover the evil messengers of death before they can strike again. While they are carrying out *their* responsibilities, *our* plan of attack is revealed in our Field Manual:

"So do not be afraid of them. There is nothing concealed that will not be disclosed, or hidden that will not be known" (Matt 10:26 NIV).

This scripture outlines our strategic agenda. First, we are to be bold. We cannot be afraid of the terrorists, as we have already seen in Chapter Two. The Church cannot be consumed with fearful praying, like "Lord, don't let me be exposed to anthrax". Yes, you can pray that, but that is a defensive prayer. We are addressing our offensive strategy against the enemy! The Church cannot let our responses be driven by fear; they must be driven by the fight!

What we are to be strategically praying is that everything that is *"concealed"* and *"hidden"* will be *"disclosed"* and made *"known"*. In other words, we are to be praying precisely that the unseen, invisible messengers of terror will be unmasked. The Church is to be providing cover for the "armorbearers" by entreating God that they will receive clues and even flashes of divine wisdom, that will set them on the path of the criminals. We are to pray specifically that the perpetrators will make a detectable mistake and be discovered *quickly*.

We should also be interceding that the location of their *"hidden"* laboratories will be made *"known"*. Then we must pray that <u>everyone</u> who is involved in cultivating bio-terror will be identified. That includes any foreign supporters, local sources, suppliers, etcetera. We are to pray against their ability to hide from authorities.

We should also make supplications against the spirit of suicide, and those who are willing to die in the killing of innocents.

Our prayers can also be made that God will set an "ambush" against the bio-terrorist, that they will be exposed to their own demonic bio-agents before they can expose anyone else.

Additionally, we are to make Spiritual requests that any bio-terrorism agents will be rendered harmless. Did you know that exposure to ultra-violet light will de-activate anthrax? Through our warfare prayer, we should expose all of these things to *The Light*!

As a result, all of the official reports will credit our armorbearers — the official law enforcement agencies with their capturing or uncovering. They will be celebrated for their hard work and diligence. They may even be recognized and rewarded for bringing the evil-doers to justice. Some may even receive medals.

And the Church will celebrate with them. But, at our altars, we will know that it was really the Spiritual activity of the Church that caused the enemies to be *"disclosed"* and made *"known"*. It was our diligence in prayer that "ambushed" and "discomfited" the enemy.

As they celebrate their *final blow*, we will quietly celebrate our *fatal blow*. Because we will know that behind it all was Spiritual activity. **It was the Church, the Lord's woman, that dropped the stone, crushing the skull of the enemy!**

"THEREFORE, WE WILL NOT FEAR,
EVEN THOUGH THE EARTH
BE REMOVED,
AND THOUGH THE MOUNTAINS
BE CARRIED INTO
THE MIDST OF THE SEA."
- PSALMS 26:2 NKJV

CHAPTER NINE

The Day The Tower Fell

A tower fell in Jesus' day. It was in the city of Siloam. Eighteen people died.

People responded *then* the same way we have responded *now* — with questions. They sought out Jesus, the most profound religious leader of the day, to ask Him the one question that still plagues us: *"Why did God let those people die?"*

If anyone could have solved that mystery it was Jesus. However, He did not give an answer to that ageless inquiry. Instead, Jesus addressed what was of far greater importance, answering the unasked question. His response was, *"Unless you repent, you will all likewise perish"* (Luke 13:5).

In the face of the tragic events, the Compassionate Healer sounded uncaring. However, hear the heart of His message.

First, Jesus is saying that death is inevitable, whether it be a tower falling, or simply going to sleep at night and not waking up.

Secondly, and most importantly, He is saying that there is only one thing that keeps death from being genuinely tragic. That is life without meaning and purpose. Having Jesus Christ as your Lord and Savior is what gives true meaning and purpose, and life in its fullness.

Without Jesus Christ, a death by any cause whatsoever is a tragedy!

If you don't have Jesus in your life, then you have every reason to be afraid. If there is nothing to hope for on the other side of this life, then we have just cause to hold on to this life so dearly.

But, for those of us who walk with Jesus, if more towers fall, or if the days become more perilous, our hope endures. For Jesus' victory over terror and death doesn't just reassure us in death, it gives us courage and strength in life. We can live everyday without "the spirit of fear".

Our national and political leaders are encouraging us to return to life as normal. Well, religious leaders cannot allow that to happen!

Christians must not return to life as normal. If we do, we will be ineffective and indifferent. We will be lax and lukewarm. We cannot revert to that.

We also cannot handle our Christianity the way we have handled it in the past. We must be fanatical! We must be zealous! We must be violent for the Kingdom!* We must be radical!

The Church cannot be *ordinary* and still make an *impact*. As the "salt" in our dull world, we cannot remain *in* the salt-shaker and make any recognizable differences. We must move out of our containers and effect the essence of our environment. (Matt 5:13)

Additionally, we cannot allow those in the world around us to 'get back to life as normal'. *Normal* was ignoring God until there was a crisis. *Normal* was prioritizing the pursuit of 'stuff' ahead of family. *Normal* was being driven by selfish desires and only thinking about the "now". Without Christ, *normal* is dangerous. With Christ, life should never be *normal* again.

Since the towers fell, these have not been normal times. So, in these abnormal times when security has been heightened, there is heightened opportunity for the Church to minister security that is only had through Jesus Christ. In this day when everyone is consumed with news reports, which lend only to fear, the Church must broadcast the Good News of God's Word. In this period when the threat of attack looms, be it bombs or bacteria, the Church must stand sure and deliver with clarity, the message that there is no fear in Jesus Christ. In this season of tragedy, pain and grief, the Church must minister healing and hope. In this era of a New War Against Terrorism, the Church must step to the battlefront and lead the fight against the demonic forces of terror and fear. And when death is on the nation's mind, only the Church can minister life!

We must minister life that cannot be crushed when towers fall. We must minister life that cannot be extinguished of dreams. We must minister life that does not end at the grave.

So even if the towers fall, you will not "perish".

* This in no way condones or encourages the terrorist attacks that so-called Christians carry out on abortion clinics, or other hurtful and harmful atrocities done in the name of Jesus.

This is the prayer that the heroes of United Airlines Flight 93 prayed just before their plane fell:

"The LORD is my shepherd;
I shall not want.
He makes me to lie down in green pastures;
He leads me beside the still waters.
He restores my soul;
He leads me in the paths of righteousness
For His name's sake.
Yea, though I walk through
the valley of the shadow of death,
I will fear no evil;
For You are with me;
Your rod and Your staff, they comfort me.
You prepare a table before me
in the presence of my enemies;
You anoint my head with oil;
My cup runs over.
Surely goodness and mercy shall follow me
All the days of my life;
And I will dwell in the house of the LORD
Forever."
- Psalms 23 NKJV

"WE ALWAYS CARRY AROUND
IN OUR BODY
THE DEATH OF JESUS,
SO THAT THE LIFE OF JESUS
MAY ALSO BE REVEALED
IN OUR BODY."
- 2 COR 4:10 NIV

CHAPTER TEN

The End or the Beginning

"Were the apocalyptic events a Biblical sign of the end of the world?" That is the question that many have asked, as we try to make sense of these events and put them into some kind of perspective.

While 'end-time prophecy' does speak of cataclysmic events as a sign of the end, the most critical sign is the one we seem to focus on the least. We are looking to Armageddon. Jesus is looking to the Church. Jesus is not coming back because the world got *so bad*. He is coming back because the Church got *so good*! The triumphant end-time return of Jesus Christ is for His Church – His "*glorious Church*"! (Eph 5:27)

If we respond properly to the occasion, this will only be the beginning – the beginning of the Church arising to its glorious purpose of representing God in the earth. Until we do that, there is no rush for Him to take us out of here.

This season is ripe to being the greatest era of the Church. If the Church were to be "caught up", taken away, or 'raptured', who would represent God in this fertile season? If the world were to end now, the devil would be the winner.

We are here <u>even now</u> for a specific purpose. This purpose is made known in a letter to the early Church: *"His intent was that now,* ***through the Church****, the manifold wisdom of God should be made known to the rulers and authorities in the heavenly realms"* (Eph 3:10 NIV).

Our nation is searching for answers to so many difficult questions. We have grave concerns and growing confusion. God has those answers to our complex issues. But God has intended for His "multifaceted wisdom" to be revealed through His glorious Church.

That is why it is so critical for the Church to step into its position and purpose *now*. The only way the world will experience that divine wisdom will be when the Church begins to reveal it. And only then will we be the glorious Church.

The Church must stop looking to the government for answers; whether it be in dealing with social issues, or soul issues. *We* have the answers *they* need! Since we have access to the wisdom of God, they should be looking to us, like the Queen of Sheba looked to King Solomon, to find answers to the perplexing questions. Notice that when the Queen of Sheba presented her *"hard questions"* to Solomon, *"Solomon answered all of her questions; nothing was too hard for the king to explain to her"* (1 Kings 10:3).

There is a *"many-sided"* divine wisdom for the many issues that we must address as a nation. God has a wisdom for war and a wisdom for those wounded by war. The glorious Church must access that *"manifold wisdom of God"* and begin to administer it on our many sides.

Significant to our becoming His "glorious Church" is the fulfilling of this scripture: *"This Gospel of the Kingdom will be preached in the whole world as a testimony to all nations, and then the end will come"* (Matt 24:14 NIV).

One complex issue that the Church must

deal with is the matter of executing a national justice in this situation, without closing the door of opportunity for preaching the gospel to that part of the world. Without His wisdom, we will win the war but lose the right to address what is at the heart of all the hatred, violence, rejection and terror.

The Church must be sensitive to deal with this issue through intercession, praying the will of God, *"Not wanting anyone to perish, but everyone to come to repentance"* (2 Peter 3:9 NIV). We must have an open door to minister the Gospel of the Kingdom to the Muslim world.

Until that happens, we must stop all of this religious talk about *the end.* We can't pack to leave until we have completed what He left us here to do. Instead of focusing on the end, we should focus on this being the beginning of a new era for His glorious Church.

And when we preach to all nations, many will *"Repent, then, and turn to God, so that your sins may be wiped out,* ***that times of refreshing may come from the Lord****"* (Acts 3:19 NIV). How we need times of refreshing.

'Refreshing' always reminds us of new beginnings.

This book has several purposes: First, it is to open eyes to the Spiritual significance of the horrific events our nation is experiencing.

Secondly, it is to provoke the Church of its glorious purpose and to call Her to "arms" against terror and fear. In so doing, I pray that each individual Christian will cast the spirit of fear out of their lives and be encouraged. That means to have courage breathed in, and only the Spirit of God can do that.

I want to stir Christians to embrace their dual personas, in the likeness of Christ, of Lion and Lamb. Against our enemies, we must be valiant warriors. But toward those who have been victimized by the enemy, we must compassionately continue the ministry of Jesus Christ. This was His mission statement:

"The Spirit of the LORD is upon Me,
Because He has anointed Me
To preach the gospel to the poor;
He has sent Me to heal the brokenhearted,
To proclaim liberty to the captives
And recovery of sight to the blind,
To set at liberty those who are oppressed;
To proclaim the acceptable year of the LORD."

- (Luke 4:18-19 NKJV)

Another purpose of this book is to bring to the awareness of those in civil authority the Church's ability to overcome terror, in this multi-faceted war, and their need to embrace our strength.

Finally, but just as important, I want to speak to the heart of anyone who may be afraid, or who is facing life with uncertainty. I want to reach out to any who have been traumatized by the recent events or any of life's events. You need to do two things: First, you must believe on the Lord Jesus Christ. To begin that process, contact a Spirit-filled church. Then become faithful as a member. No soldier should be on the battlefield alone.

If this book satisfies its mission, we will not be victimized by fear and terror, or gripped by anxiety and held captive by our imaginations. We will be able to see the once-invisible enemy and rise victoriously over those demonic forces and all of their dastardly weapons. We will move from fear to faith to freedom!

I close with a very personal note. The writing of this book has been a burden to me (Zech 12:1). It was written in obedience to these explicit orders (which also explains my unique qualifications to give the charges that I do):

"When you are about to go into battle, the priest shall come forward and address the army.

He shall say: "Hear, O [my people], today you are going into battle against your enemies.

Do not be fainthearted or afraid; do not be terrified or give way to panic before them.

For the LORD your God is the one who goes with you to fight for you against your enemies to give you victory." (Deuteronomy 20:1-4 NIV)

So, today I step into my responsibility to call the Church to step into theirs.

Likewise I remind our civil leaders and encourage our conventional forces to be brave, but do not try to fight this battle alone. The Church must be with you, *then* the Lord will fight for you.

Church, we had been ignored, but now we must arrive on the scene like the calvary in an old Western movie. **We *are* the calvary because of Calvary!**

We will conquer fear and terror. For the Lord will be with us! And we will be victorious over **The Invisible Enemy**. Then the freedom of our soil and our soul will be enduring!

"THROUGH THE BLESSING
OF THE UPRIGHT
A CITY IS EXALTED."

- PROVERBS 11:11 NIV

GOD BLESS AMERICA

"RIGHTEOUSNESS EXALTS A NATION,
BUT SIN IS A DISGRACE
TO ANY PEOPLE."

- PROVERBS 14:34 NIV

Acknowledgments

These individuals lent their abilities and their encouragement to provoke this work to completion:

First, to Dr. E. Marlene Hunt, my brilliant and beautiful wife, and the real writer and warrior in the family. She is my encouragement to write, my editor and my wordsmith.

Next, to Bishop Frederick Hightower, who confirmed the message, and who *first* told the Church to raise its shield. Then to Ed McAteer, whose energy opened doors for this message .

To my two sisters—on by birth, Gayle D. Hunt, and the other by thievery, Jacqueline G. McCreight. They devoted hours to reading the manuscript and many more hours to encourage me to complete this work.

To Celia Rocks of Rocks-DeHart Public Relations. Her strategy and planning saved this preacher, then set me on the right path. She gave wings to my message. Also, to Craig Thompson at Disciple Design whose creativity has added strength to many of my projects!

Selwyn E. Hunt, the 'bestest' brother in the whole world, and Angela P. King, my outstanding sister-in-law, both offered valuable insights that helped me in the expression of this message.

I value the input of Pastor Craig John Ferguson, who shared the burden of this message with me, and Annette Jacobs, "the reader". They are both members of the Spiritual Special Ops.

Finally, I owe a debt to my parents, Gary and Ethel Hunt. They have always believed in me. And to the members of the wonderful church I am privileged to pastor, Abundant Grace! They said "Amen" to this message.